UNLOCKING YOUR PURPOSE TO LIVE YOUR BEST LIFE

A 31 DAY JOURNAL

APRIL HOLT SMITH

DEDICATION

This book is dedicated to my best, lovely and adorable friend, Gloretta (Gege) King. Amazingly, you have been my trusted, reliable and dependable confidant for over twenty years. Like a pillar, Glorretta stood by me through the good and bad times, supporting and pushing me to be the best I could be.

Gege, you're more like my sister than a friend. At tough and demanding juncture of life when I felt weak, discouraged and wanted to give up, you always told me, "April, you can do this, keep pushing".

Back then, when I used to get upset with people that I thought should support and believe in my dream, but they didn't, you would often say, "What have I told you about that girl?" Thank you for being my number one cheerleader, sister and best friend. I appreciate your invaluable encouragement and motivation; you have immensely contributed to my growth. Gloretta (Gege) King, I love you.

Contents

INTRODUCTION

The strength of any purposeful life stems from the ability to recognize, unlock and consistently work towards the fulfillment of such purpose. Dreams, visions and wishes are unlimited, but fulfillment is as rare as gold. Almost every woman has good and enviable dreams, but it is saddening that fewer women succeed and actualize their set goals.

Failure to actualize ones vision, talent and calling is traceable to this fact, vision demands our relentless commitment before it can be achieved. Realistically, until you deliberately make remarkable contributions to your purpose, living a successful life will remain a mirage.

Though our generation has been branded 'fortunate generation", many thanks to technological advancement and numerous innovations, yet many people still find it difficult to fulfill their dreams, pathetically, they live and die unnoticed. The reason for their ineffectiveness and inactivity is solely connected to their failure to discover, strategize and live out their God-given purposes. Be informed, fulfillment is like a sparkling beam of light, it will naturally announce itself – nobody can conceal it.

Evidently, this journal is a potent tool that will promptly help you in discovering, recovering and actualizing your purpose. Also, it is the master key that will unlock and grant you access to realms of unspeakable blessings. Additionally, it will propel you to fight the good fight of purpose; subsequently, you will live a life guaranteed of daily victory, success, breakthrough and accomplishment of purpose, as well as crown your head with golden diadem of fulfillment.

I pray that the Holy Spirit will breathe on you as you journey through the pages of this journal. I urge you to adhere strictly to all instructions and offer the prayers contained in this life changing journal.

DAY ONE
DISCOVER YOURSELF

Scriptural text: Man that is in honor, and understandeth not, is like the beasts that perish (Ps. 49:20).

The Scripture above is a precursor to fulfillment of purpose, because until a woman discovers herself, living a confused life is inevitable. The biblical story of King Nebuchadnezzar is an ancient proof that when anybody loses his or her sense, the person is bound to behave irrationally. Surprisingly, the day Nebuchadnezzar's understanding returned to him, his reign as king resumed immediately.

The story of the prodigal son is another example that clearly reveals that self discovery is pivotal to fulfillment of purpose. This young man was already eating with swine, but when he came to his senses, he reasoned that many servants in his father's house lived and enjoyed life than he was doing in a strange land. Therefore, he rightly thought and concluded in his heart that he will return to his father to plead for mercy and acceptance despite his reckless and riotous life.

This unprofitable son discovered his worth and position was in contrast with his present experience. Graciously, he quickly retraced his step, got back on track and regained his lofty position. Undoubtedly, until a woman discovers herself, such an individual will remain irrelevant, unproductive and unfulfilled.

Dinah was completely ignorant of her worth, status and significance; hence, she became a victim of sexual abuse. She was pure and pretty, greatly blessed with qualities that generations should admire and covet. Pathetically, she was blind to her glory, dignity and virtue.

Dinah was created to be the envy of many nations and generations after her. She was the only female child among many sons; the apple of her parents' eyes and the pride of her valiant brothers. Unfortunately, she drifted from been celebrated as a rare gem to an object of war and destruction. She embarked on an ignoble trip to see the indecent ladies of a polluted land and her purpose was truncated.

Reflection: If you don't discover yourself, you will abuse your purpose.

Prayer Point: Father, open the eyes of my understanding to discover myself.

Note:_____

_____

_____

_____

_____

_____

DAY TWO
YOU ARE A SPECIAL VESSEL

Scriptural text: *The glory of this latter house shall be greater than of the former, saith the Lord of hosts: and in this place will I give peace, saith the Lord of hosts* ***(Hag. 2:9).***

I t is not unusual to observe the latter is often superior to the former. Woman is a latter creature while man is a former creature.

And the Lord God said, it is not good that the man should be alone; I will make him a help meet for him ***(Gen. 2:18).***

Women are not products of biological accident or mistake; instead, they are unique, exceptional and excellent beings. Wise and observant people have opined that there are certain things that men do can be done more excellently by women.

Women are epitome of prudence; this truth is substantiated by their frugality, managerial and exceptional management skills. Things that seem insufficient in the hands of men would be much more abundant when given to women. Arguably, women are more observant, meticulous, precise and accurate than men. Therefore, if these virtues are properly utilized and maximized by women, it will precipitate inexplicable success and jaw-dropping achievement.

Considering the order of creation, woman came after man, who is the original symbol of strength and dominion.

Women are latter species with inner vigor and vibrancy. The strength of women is not physical power like that of men, but it is hidden, and it takes conscious and deliberate effort to unveil it.

Always remember that the glory of the latter shall exceed the former. Like wine, women are sweet, sound, sparkling, rich, honorable, desirable and acceptable. Let this mind be in you as it was in valuable women of old.

Reflection: Women are fearfully and wonderfully made. They deserve honor, respect and care.

Prayer point: I receive grace to live as a special vessel unto honor that brings glory to God at all times.

Note:_____

_____

_____

_____

_____

_____

DAY THREE
YOU ARE COMPLETE

Scriptural text: And the Lord God said, it is not good that the man should be alone; I will make him a help meet for him (Gen. 2:18).

Prior to the emergence of Eve at creation, it was repeatedly stated that everything created by God was good. In fact, goodness almost became a cliché before God commented that Adam was incomplete, because there was a conspicuous vacuum in his life. On this note, God declared that the state of his existence was incomplete.

It is an unarguable fact that, what is missing in all men was injected, enclosed and inundated in women. Structurally, women are symbols of beauty and visible representation of perfection. There is no doubt that women are complete in Jesus.

And ye are complete in him, which is the head of all principality and power (Col. 2:10).

Again, it is an indisputable fact that if women are brought to any scene of confusion and chaos, their witty presence will activate tranquility, calmness and clarity will descend like dew from above. During the biblical era, the whole Jewish race faced imminent and raging destruction orchestrated by an influential enemy - Haman; thereby the entire Jewish race were despaired with little or no hope of survival.

Graciously, when the Jews were disturbingly perplexed, a glorious woman (Queen Esther) was raised by God to appease the king and pacify him to change his decision. This task was risky and indeed enormous, but it was not a surprise that only a woman could execute it. All men did their best, they fasted and prayed, but only a woman was able to appear before the king. Truly, she did what men could not do.

Women's power rarely fails. Expectedly, Queen Esther won the favor of the king; she defeated the purpose of their arch enemy as she quietly got unassailable victory and consequently redeemed the lives of her people. She wonderfully executed the plan and ultimate desire of the elders. Indeed, there is completion anointing on women.

It is visible that sometimes when men are stranded, sweating, struggling and battered, women are surprisingly strong, shinning, standing and unperturbed. If women are allowed, they have all the requirements to change the world for good.

Reflection: There is something in you that fills the vacuum in your world.

Prayer point: Henceforth, I activate the completion anointing upon my life. No more incomplete project, abandonment and delay in Jesus' name.

Note:_____

_____

_____

_____

DAY FOUR
YOU ARE A MOTHER

Scriptural text: *The inhabitants of the villages ceased, they ceased in Israel, until that I Deborah arose, that I arose a mother in Israel* **(Judg. 5:7).**

Abraham, the father of faith almost failed in executing his divine purpose. He was afraid of King Abimelech, but Sarah the mother of all women stood her ground to face the situation alone when her lord (husband) almost forsook her. Thereafter, her courage cum victory flowed down to faithful women of all ages.

The mystery of motherhood is neither concealed in verbal power nor biological fruitfulness; rather it is an inner quality that produces visible results. Deborah selflessly sought the good of other people, especially the helpless. One of the common characteristics of any good mother is her preference for good and comfort of her children and dependants. Sarah's defense of Abraham is a classical example of the role a good mother must play in the life of their family members.

Be informed, until you learn and as well begin to put others first you may not discover your purpose. One of the easiest ways to discover your purpose and talent is by serving others. When you care and seek to solve the problems of other people you will unknowingly solve your own problem. It is not mere imagination or vain thought that, when you strive to solve certain problems, you stand great chance of unfolding your hidden abilities. David killed the monstrous enemy called Goliath, and this singular feat paved way for his enthronement.

Motherhood transcends the period of child birth, nurturing and training. It is an act of giving direction to chaotic situations and difficult circumstances of life. Mother Deborah drastically changed the name of the feeble Israelites to champions, bound nation to boundless country, the besieged to triumphant citizens, prisoners to preservers, beggars to givers, weaklings to winners and depressed people to joyful singers.

You are a great mother created to be enjoyed by countless people from different nations of the world, not to be endured by anyone. You are to be desired not to be disserted. Remember that you are created in the order of Matriarchs of faith, loved and enjoyed by all and sundry.

Today, you can become a good and reputable mother. Stop searching for men to help you, your family, nation or immediate society, because you are purposely created to fix problems.

Reflection: Fathers may fail in performing their duties, but mothers cannot forget their sucking children.

Prayer point: Almighty God, make me a good mother and role model to nations of the world.

Note:_____

_____

_____

_____

DAY FIVE
PURPOSE AND TIME

Scriptural text: *To every thing there is a season, and a time to every purpose under the heaven* **(Eccl. 3:1)**.

Purpose and time are intertwined; every purpose has an accomplishment time attached to it. In your quest for fulfillment, every time is not your time. All women were not born the same day and all of them cannot die the same day.

What you do as a woman is as significant as when you do it. Doing the right thing at the wrong time is still the same as doing the wrong thing. If you fail in your timing, you will fulfillment. Time and purpose must synchronize before our aim, purpose and goal could be achieved.

It is impossible to live forever, only God is ageless. Endeavor to make every time count, even a second. Time is not renewable; once you lose it, it is lost forever. A wasted time is a wasted purpose and a wasted purpose is an abuse of destiny. Wasting your time is equivalent to truncating your purpose.

Time and strength obey the law of diminishing return. At a certain period of life, you have huge amount of time to invest into your purpose and this opportunity keeps increasing until later in life when time and strength will begin to dwindle.

According to wise people, "Time is money". Therefore stop wasting your precious time, instead, endeavor to invest it. Pleasure is good, but when it becomes the hallmark of life, fulfillment of purpose suffers setback.

Develop a healthy culture of saving time the same way you save money, and the best way to save time is to invest it in your purpose. What you do with your time will define the outcome of your life.

Jacob, the favorite of God was flooded with promises, yet he was very conscious of time at every point of his life. He said, "When will I prepare for my home?" He knew that timely fulfillment is far better, if he lacked this important knowledge, his purpose will wither. It is impossible to fulfill destiny without mastering the laws of time.

"Work when you ought to work and play when you ought to play" is the golden rule that guarantees success. Always remember that it is too late to cry when the head is off the neck; therefore make hay when the sun shines. Sleeping when you ought to be at work will make any woman to restlessly be at work when she ought to be resting. There is no 120 years old woman in any part of the world that has equal strength and vigor of a healthy female teenager, therefore be wise.

Reflection: What must I start doing in order to fulfill my purpose?

Prayer point: I receive grace to judiciously utilize my time.

Note:_____

_____

_____

DAY SIX
THE POWER OF SELF-ESTEEM

Scriptural text: *And Caleb stilled the people before Moses, and said, let us go up at once, and possess it; for we are well able to overcome it. And there we saw the giants, the sons of Anak, which come of the giants: and we were in our own sight as grasshoppers, and so we were in their sight* **(Num. 13:30, 33)**.

Today's Scriptural text gives an interesting account of two different sets of people chosen to represent their country. They were saddled with the responsibility of spying a land and reporting their findings to their leader – Moses.

The first party saw themselves as great and capable people, endowed with the ability to suppress and totally subdue any opposition irrespective of its fierceness. These men, Caleb and Joshua, possessed understanding and carry the true image of God. They were determined and dauntless in their approach, because they knew their worth and ability in God. They knew that with God's support, one man can conquer a nation.

It is quite pathetic to note that the other party had higher number of people, but they were men of blurred vision and dwarf self-image. These bunch of feeble minds thoughtlessly and frightfully declared that they were like grasshoppers. True to their words, they hopped and died like grasshoppers in the wilderness.

It is a basic law of life, either physical or spiritual that, your thought is your life. Pessimism and optimism are primary determinants of human's results. You can't grow an inch above your thoughts. The surest barrier of purpose is low mentality and poor self-image.

Until you disclose your case as closed, it is broadly open. Who you are inside will define who you will be outside. Proper self image or self identification is the solid foundation of any glorious destiny. The way you define yourself will determine how the world will define you, because situation and circumstances will definitely conform to your inward resolution.

You can afford to miss some physical opportunities in life and still forge ahead to succeed. But you cannot afford to have a defective inner picture of yourself and taste success. Whatever a woman thinks in her heart that is what she becomes.

Reflection: Blind eye is better than blind mind.

Prayer point: O Lord, open the eyes of my heart that I may see your wonderful plans for my life.

Note:_____

_____

_____

_____

_____

_____

DAY SEVEN
UNFORGIVENESS: KILLER OF PURPOSE

Scriptural text: *For if ye forgive men their trespasses, your heavenly Father will also forgive you: but if ye forgive not men their trespasses, neither will your Father forgive your trespasses* **(Matt. 6:14-15).**

Jesus was sent to save the world; but the world rejected and despised His ministry. Consequently, they apprehended Him, leveled false allegations against Him, and ultimately, He was crucified. Nonetheless, the Jesus Christ forgave the world in order to fulfill His glorious purpose.

Joseph was ordained to liberate His family from hunger and as well preserve the nation of Egypt and the whole world from famine. His brothers maltreated him and sold him to a strange land – Egypt. Additionally, in his passionate pursuit of his purpose, despite his discouraging experiences, he joyously interpreted the dream of a forgetful butler. Amazingly, Joseph forgave all his offenders in order to fulfill his enviable purpose.

Moses was the spiritual giant sent to deliver the nation of Israel from their prolonged captivity. He attempted to fight for them, but they rejected him. He went on exile to save his dear life, yet he was ready to die for them when he returned from his forty years exile. Over and above all, despite their rebellion, at a certain time he was ready to surrender his eternal rest for their restoration and fulfillment.

Time and space will preclude me from discussing Stephen, who uttered prayer of forgiveness to win eternal crown as the first Christian martyr. Father, forgive them because they don't know what they are doing. Father, never count this sin against them is the heart cries of people that will fulfill purpose.

Until you learn to heartily forgive your friends, spouse, associates, relatives, etc, you are not qualify to taste greatness. Don't forget that an enemy today can become a friend tomorrow. As nights turn to days, people's character can evolve and become better. Apostle Paul was once a terrific persecutor, who masterminded the killing of innocent Stephen, but later, he died for the same course he once vehemently fought against.

Reflection: If I forgive others, I will receive forgiveness and fly higher in the flight of destiny.

Prayer point: Father, take away the heart of stone and help me to forgive all my offenders.

Note:_____

_____

_____

_____

_____

_____

DAY EIGHT
LET THE PAST BE PAST

Scriptural text: *Remember ye not the former things, neither consider the things of old. Behold, I will do a new thing; now it shall spring forth; shall ye not know it? I will even make a way in the wilderness, and rivers in the desert* **(Is. 43:18-19).**

Past is an irreparable event. Dwelling on the past is dying without knowing. God will never consider our past to determine our future. Start doing the right thing today and you will amazingly begin to get jaw-dropping results. You can't do anything to influence the past, but you can only lay hold on the present to enhance the future.

Human beings are imperfect being; they are liable to making mistakes at one stage or the other. But what you do with your mistakes will determine the excellence of your life or otherwise. Occasional blunders and errors are inevitable in your quest for growth and development, but perpetual mistakes are indicators of being impervious, insensitive and complacent about your life and purpose.

Wise people continuously learn from their shortcomings, while unwise people are temporal thinkers. They show brief remorse for their errors, but continually return to their vomit. Nothing teaches and strengthens better than the past if properly engaged.

You are clearly instructed not to remember the past, because it is already on the irrecoverable side of life. The past is dead, let its pain and memory also die. If you don't allow the past to be past, its flood may displace you. Excessive consideration of pain and past is equivalent to celebration of weakness and ignorance.

Until you let go of the past, you will never see a new dawn. In every old tale there is a new thing to learn or gain. Every pain has a gain enclosed in it. Interestingly, it is often said that pain is the precursor of gain. Besides, every coin has dual sides and you are bound to witness the other side of your pain, which is goodness. Truly, your joy, hope, help, health, wealth, fame, connection, reign, progress, access and success shall spring forth.

Reflection: If I let go, I shall be let loose.

Prayer point: I declare, my season of new beginning has come.

Note:_____

_____

_____

_____

_____

_____

DAY NINE
LOVE YOURSELF

*Scriptural text: For no man ever yet hated his own flesh; but nourisheth and cherisheth it, even as the Lord the church: for we are members of his body, of his flesh, and of his bones **(Eph. 5:29-30)**.*

Self love is paramount to success as well as fulfillment of purpose. If you hate yourself, you will eventually think that the whole world hates you. But you should bear in mind that there is no woman on earth that is hated by everyone. There is something in you that certain people love and cherish, therefore love yourself.

You are not as bad as you may think, if people detest your look, they may desire your lifestyle, talent or resources. You cannot be bad without something good about your life. Jephthah was hated by his own family members and maliciously driven away from home, but people in the society later loved him for his courage and inexplicable strength.

There is a crown that fits your head, a throne that awaits you and lovers that love you like their own soul. Please, love yourself, because if you don't love yourself nobody will love or appreciate you. Again, the way you present yourself will dictate the degree of societal acceptance you will enjoy. Whatever you call yourself is what the world will call you.

Your self-love has a great deal of influence on your value, and your value will determine your worth. Emphatically, it is an abomination for any woman to dislike herself.

You belong to the Lord; you are part of His bone and flesh. You have the exact feature and nature of God. If God is comely, you are equally comely, if He is wise, then you have great capacity for wisdom, if He is powerful, you are strong and if God is holy, you can be holy like Him. Apostle Paul revealed that we have the righteousness of God. It is not an exaggeration that you have the propensity to completely reflect God's glory, because you are created in His glorious image.

Reflection: I cannot hate myself and expect others to love me. Henceforth, I will love myself unconditionally.

Prayer point: Father, bestow me with the grace to love myself.

Note:_____

_____

_____

_____

_____

_____

DAY TEN
LOVE YOUR NEIGHBOR

Scriptural text: And the second is like unto it, thou shalt love thy neighbor as thyself. On these two commandments hang all the law and the prophets (Matt. 22:39-40).

The highest level of spiritual maturity is love. If you master the act of love you have mastered the greatest requirement of God. Staying in love is like living in eternity. If you crave for love, God will warmly love you. Sincerely, God doesn't demand any other thing from you other than love.

It is surprising that all the laws of the Holy Bible are premised on love. If only you can love other people like yourself, you are free from the pain and plague of sin. Similarly, if you love your neighbor like yourself you will enjoy all the exceedingly great promises of God.

Affirmatively, love is everything. Love doesn't fail and it cannot fail; it is as powerful as death (Song of Sol. 8:6-7). A number of people are failing in life, because they refuse to love wholeheartedly. Love will work and reign till eternity.

Love was the only sacrifice that saved the world and it remains the only therapy that can salvage purpose. In any generation, failure, frustration, evil and unfulfillment will disturbingly increase until affection is embraced. Summarily, Jesus gave us two commandments and the commandments are hinged on love. Any purpose that is not established in love will surely end in obscurity.

Dorcas was promptly redeemed from the power of the grave, because of her visible demonstration of love. She was suddenly gripped by death, but the people that felt the impact of her love called for spiritual help and she was raised back to life.

Reflection: Love is immortal and any love driven-purpose is indestructible.

Prayer point: I receive the grace to affectionately show love to people in Jesus' name.

Note:_____

_____

_____

_____

_____

_____

DAY ELEVEN
MASTERING RELATIONSHIPS

Scriptural text: *Awake to righteousness, and sin not; for some have not the knowledge of God: I speak this to your shame* *(1 Cor. 15:34).*

People may look alike in structure, yet it should be noted that they differ in exposure, nature and character. There is no doubt that one man's meat is another man's poison; therefore there is an urgent need to learn better ways of relating with people of different behaviors.

It is absolutely impossible to fulfill destiny in isolation. Every good purpose must be people oriented, and if people are not carefully handled, purpose will become futile. It is interesting that people that studied Animal Science or Veterinary Medicine will still need human beings to bring animals to them for treatment.

The ultimate purpose of Deborah was to deliver Israel from oppression, howbeit she related perfectly with elders, men and women. Moses was highly skilled in managing people. He was blameless before Jethro, the Midianite and all his children. He humbly tendered his animals for many decades and he was successful in relating with human beings and animals alike. Finally, Moses was a great leader that successfully led the stubborn nation of Israel for forty years.

Failure in relationship will automatically birth failure of purpose. When you are in harmony with people, fulfillment of purpose will be enhanced. But if otherwise, actualization of dream becomes a mirage. You need people to fulfill purpose, because only you cannot make the recognition, fulfillment and celebration of your purpose count.

Your impact will be felt in accordance to the quality of your relationship with people. You should recall that Paul almost lost larger portion of his ministry to soiled relationship. Angrily, he parted with Barnabas, who was divinely called and commissioned with him. Besides, during another season of conflict of opinion, he almost lost Mark his useful follower.

This is my submission, only God could predict the level of success that Paul and Barnabas would have recorded if they worked together as ordained by God.

Reflection: Good relationship is a currency; it has equal purchasing power with money.

Prayer point: Help me O Lord to value people in Jesus' name.

Note:_____

_____

_____

_____

_____

_____

DAY TWELVE
ENGAGE DIVINE AUTHORITY

Scriptural text: Verily I say unto you, whatsoever ye shall bind on earth shall be bound in heaven; and whatsoever ye shall loose on earth shall be loosed in heaven (Matt. 18:18).

Nothing could be greater than the limitless authority given to sons and daughters of God. God is not man that He would tell lies and He is not the son of man that He would give and revoke. All the gifts of God are irrevocable, therefore you are who God says you are and you possess whatever He declared as yours.

Any daughter of God who is currently living under oppression is only oppressed by her ignorance and any daughter of God that lacks good things willingly chose to live as pauper. Your new birth conferred unlimited power on you, therefore you have unlimited authority over visible and invisible things.

Jesus did not only come to this world to redeem you, He equally came to demonstrate how to walk in dominion. Throughout His earthly ministry, Jesus lived victoriously on every side. Therefore, He clearly declared to His disciples that as the Father sent Him, He is also sending them. This implies that you are entitled to everything He has and you are sent to do everything He did, and to even do more. Everything that worked for Jesus will work for you and everything under Him is also under you.

And Jesus came and spake unto them, saying, all power is given unto me in heaven and in earth. Go ye therefore, and teach all nations, baptizing them in the name of the Father, and of the Son, and of the Holy Ghost: teaching them to observe all things whatsoever I have commanded you: and, lo, I am with you alway, even unto the end of the world **(Matt. 28:18-20)**.

This is the farewell message of Jesus to every member of His body – the church, and it is a promissory note of power and authority. You have everything at your finger tip. Like the Prophets of old, you can do and undo through the power of God at work in your life.

Henceforth, you should talk and act like a woman that has authority, because you have it indeed.

Reflection: If I decree a thing, it shall be established, because I have unquestionable authority in God.

Prayer point: Henceforth, none of my words shall fall to the ground in Jesus' name.

Note:_____

_____

_____

_____

_____

_____

DAY THIRTEEN
KEEP YOUR TRACK

Scriptural text: *As every man hath received the gift, even so minister the same one to another, as good stewards of the manifold grace of God. If any man speak, let him speak as the oracles of God; if any man minister, let him do it as of the ability which God giveth; that God in all things may be glorified through Jesus Christ: to whom be praise and dominion forever and ever* *(1 Pet. 4:10-11)*.

The dynamism and diversity of life is the beauty of life. It is imperative that every woman maintains her path in all issues of life. Just imagine that the whole citizens of a nation are physicians, what would happen? The entire population will be hale and hearty? No, because there is no farmer. Obviously, the same dreaded sickness will cripple a vast number of people due to malnutrition. The economy will boom and blossom? No, because there is no investor. There will be good road and edifice across the nation? No, because there is no architect. Their cities will be attractive? No, because there is no town, urban and environmental planners.

God will only reward you for doing the right thing. Doing another person's job will only bring failure and frustration, while running in another person's track will lead to disqualification. Therefore, you are mandated to maintain your own lane.

Realistically, as a visionary woman, you should always remember that what you are trained to do will never commensurate with what you are destined to do. Kindly do all you could to discover your purpose and endeavor to invest your all into it. You cannot win the race by breaking the rule, keep to your lane.

Lastly, I heard an exceedingly great man of God narrating the story of his past failure in ministry. He publicly disclosed how he emptied his bank account to finance a crusade. Shortly after the crusade, he discovered that no single soul was added to his church after the elaborate crusade.

Thereafter, he went to God in intense prayer to notify Him about his expectation and the fruitless effort he experienced. Graciously, God spoke to him in clear terms that he was not called to stage any revival, crusade or open air crusade. This great shepherd was specifically told that he was called into the teaching ministry not open air crusade. This golden instruction set the pace for his accelerated growth, greatness and advancement in ministry.

Reflection: Winners are not rules breaker, pursue your purpose lawfully.

Prayer point: Holy Spirit, order my steps and give me an obedient heart.

Note:_____

_____

_____

_____

DAY FOURTEEN
WHAT IS HOLDING YOU BACK?

Scriptural text: *What shall we then say to these things? If God be for us, who can be against us? (Rom. 8:31).*

There is nothing in heaven or earth that can hold us back from fulfilling our God given purpose. Since the advent Christ, one of the major enemies of our purpose is self. Our redemption package is complete, because the power of God in us has given us everything that pertains to life and godliness, but self is one of the factors that can hinder you from achieving your purpose.

What could stop you from attaining God's purpose? Is it sin, tribulation, distress, persecution, famine, nakedness, peril, war, economic recession, government policy, demons, diabolical powers, relatives, spouse, children, influential people, education or inflation? It is evident that none of these is strong enough to set you back.

However, the only set back you may experience would be the one initiated by you. There is no negativity in God's dictionary. Besides, believers have been empowered by God to effectively resist the devil, because the word of God has commanded you to do so. Therefore, no visible or invisible force is capable of trampling or truncating our purpose.

Above all, failure, inability, insufficiency or impossibility is never a factor to consider when you are in the center of God's will. The word of God confirms that His word will never return to Him void, without fulfilling what God sent it to do. Therefore you are not a candidate of failure and setback.

In conclusion, Paul revealed that effectual fervent door was opened to him, but there were many adversaries. Despite the huge number of his visible and invisible enemies, at the end of his life, he affirmed that he had fought the good fight of faith and equally finished his course in a grand style with eternal crown waiting for him. Confidently, he was contemplating whether to depart from this world or not after fulfilling his purpose (Phil. 1:21-24). Fear of death together with confrontations was never a threat to hold him back from fulfilling destiny.

Reflection: How have I been inhibiting my purpose?

Prayer point: I receive grace to scale every barrier obstructing the fulfillment of my purpose in Jesus' name.

Note:_____

_____

_____

_____

_____

_____

DAY FIFTEEN
BUILD YOUR ALTAR

*Scriptural text: O God, thou art my God; early will I seek thee: my soul thirsteth for thee, my flesh longeth for thee in a dry and thirsty land, where no water is; to see thy power and thy glory, so as I have seen thee in the sanctuary (**Ps. 63:1-2**).*

Altar denotes meeting point with divinity. In ancient times, any place of contact with God is often called an altar. It was believed that any time people return to that meeting point God will be ready to visit them again.

The greatest mistake of humanity is that people only seek God with seriousness and alertness when they are in dire need. However, there are parallel differences between divinity and humanity, because while human beings are craving to receive succor and blessings from God, divinity constantly desires intimate relationship with believers.

One of the surest things that are pleasant to God is true fellowship and unrestricted relationship. There is no doubt that God frequently desires to speak to you, but most believers are desperate to receive than relate with God.

The thoughts of God are different and His ways are far higher than yours. Therefore, you must be ready to tarry in His presence in order to please Him and as well secure your comfort.

The greatest people in the Bible were addicted seekers of God not receivers of physical things. Moses desperately wanted to see God's face. Therefore, he constantly had fellowship with God. No wonder, he became a power chamber with unequalled authority.

Daniel was equally noted for his uncompromised fellowship with God. It was amazing that his firm relationship with God became a snare against him. It is good to note that the national conspiracy was futile when launched against his unbreakable fellowship with God. Oh! His holy fellowship made him a friend of hungry lions. Indeed, true altars will produce extraordinary results.

Reflection: When was the last time you had a deep, rich and unforgettable fellowship with God?

Prayer point: Father, draw me close to you and give me a heart of fellowship in Jesus' name.

Note:_____

_____

_____

_____

_____

_____

DAY SIXTEEN
BREAKING BARRIERS OF PURPOSE

Scriptural text: *And it shall come to pass in that day, that his burden shall be taken away from off thy shoulder, and his yoke from off thy neck, and the yoke shall be destroyed because of the anointing **(Is. 10:27)**.*

It is no news that good things attract enemies. Personally, I regard barriers and enemies of purposes as good enemies, because they are propellers and enhancers of fulfillment.

In the race of life and purpose, everything works together for good for God's own people. Ten brothers of Joseph ganged up against him, aside domestic provocation of his step mothers. Yet he was triumphant over them. Interestingly, the day God began to show him his purpose was the day God anointed him with the gift of dreams and interpretation.

Similarly, every vision we receive from God will attract corresponding anointing. Conversely, the day God activated the fulfillment process of Joseph's destiny was the day his brothers conspired and sold him to slave trader.

Any path without challenges is not worth treading. In the same way, any purpose without opposition is not a genuine purpose. After the anointing of David, Lion, Bear, Goliath and King Saul relentlessly challenged his purpose. Praise God! Despite all the clusters of enemies against him, David prevailed.

Barriers were built by enemies because purpose is panacea in nature. Therefore, any true purpose will start and end with varieties of barriers. Jesus the King of glory was trailed by opposition. Immediately he was born, a tyrant called Herod violently rose against Him; hence, Baby Jesus was maliciously taken to the land Egypt. Later, He began His ministry and Satan monitored Him to the mountain of prayer with persistent showers of bullet targeted against dangerous aspects of his life. Additionally, the Scribes, Pharisees and Sadducees became daily thorns in His flesh. Lastly, He was not left without attacks in the grave; in fact, that was His hottest battle – The ultimate battle of purpose. Indeed, it was the final battle.

Hallelujah! There was abundant release of anointing that guaranteed His victory in these contests. In the same vein, there is need for you to crush your barriers and God has given you the required power to bend, break, blow and bow your obstacles.

Reflection: There is no barrier capable of stopping your purpose when you align with God's will.

Prayer point: I shall fulfill my purpose in Jesus' name.

Note:_____

_____

_____

_____

_____

_____

DAY SEVENTEEN
YOU ARE A HEROINE

Scriptural text: *Now the Lord had said unto Abram, get thee out of thy country, and from thy kindred, and from thy father's house, unto a land that I will show thee: and I will make of thee a great nation, and I will bless thee, and make thy name great; and thou shalt be a blessing: and I will bless them that bless thee, and curse him that curseth thee: and in thee shall all families of the earth be blessed **(Gen. 12:1-3)**.*

The making of women is quite similar to that of men. If there are heroes there must be heroines and if men are rising, it is incumbent on women to rise and shine like the sun of the noon day. Sarah was the wife of Abraham; nonetheless, she became a heroine. Any position or vocation ordained by God always leads to lofty enthronement.

Scripturally, father Abraham was specially called with divine mandate through an audible encounter to become the father of nations, yet the call of Sarah was unique and equally great, but unpronounced. Thanks to God for the resilient and resolute life of Sarah who patiently maintained the right path to become a heroine of faith. You may not hear special voice from heaven but I am assuring you that you have capacity to become a heroine and generational point of reference.

Even as Sarah obeyed Abraham, calling him lord: whose daughters ye are, as long as ye do well, and are not afraid with any amazement **(1 Pet. 3:6)**.

Sarah did not have special call, but she had special character.

- ✓ She was obedient to higher authority.

- ✓ She respected and honored her superior.

- ✓ She was addicted to godly service.

- ✓ She was courageous.

- ✓ She was not perturbed by negative situations.

You should endeavor to take these points to heart and apply them. Heaven and earth may fail, but none of these virtues will fail. Remember, there is no great woman without great character. Every success recorded was hinged on great habit. You may get other things by chance, but good name and enduring legacy is not secured by chance.

Sarah did the needful and she consequently got an eternal name for herself. In the same manner, if you adhere to these truths, you will surely become a societal model, as well as excel in all you do.

Reflection: Character is the backbone of success. Any success without strong character will end up in disgrace.

Prayer point: Father, I receive the grace to live an exemplary life in Jesus' name.

Note:_____

_____

_____

_____

DAY EIGHTEEN
THE LAW OF PROCESS

Scriptural text: *Because to every purpose there is time and judgment, therefore the misery of man is great upon him **(Pro. 8:6)**.*

Obeying the law of process is pivotal in all issues of purpose. What women are doing is as important as how they are doing it. Putting a square peg in a round hole will never lead to success of any kind in the race of destiny.

God is not haphazard; He is decent and orderly in all His doings. Therefore, any woman that will fulfill her purpose must learn how to follow due process. The way you do things will naturally predict your outcome.

Disorderliness is a sign of ungodliness. Doing things without organization is an indication of deviation from purpose. Good intention without good decision is self deception that will lead to ultimate destruction of purpose.

God is not a rewarder of ordinary workers or mere seekers; instead, He is a rewarder of diligent and committed seekers. There is need for women to consciously learn and follow acceptable processes and procedure. Avoidance of precepts is synonymous with neglect of purpose.

There is no shortcut to fulfillment of purpose. Any seeming shortcut will unavoidably shorten, shatter and scatter your enviable purpose. Remember that purpose is similar to living things; hence you need to nurture it in order to attain maturity. Every purpose starts with demand before ending up in meaningful supply.

Purpose is firm and the process of attaining it is fixed. One of the fundamental things to learn about your purpose is its laws. The rules and regulations of each purpose differ from one another. The diets, laws and skills of footballers are quite different from that of wrestlers.

The purpose of Uzzah was destroyed because he violated the precept and procedure of purpose. He attempted to jump the protocol of God and he paid for it. Be wise in all your dealings, you should not attempt to change what shouldn't be changed, because some things are fixed in nature. Attempting to facilitate fulfillment of purpose by jumping rules will automatically truncate such purpose.

Reflection: Every purpose must obey the law of process.

Prayer point: Father, I receive the grace to patiently obey the law of process in Jesus' name.

Note:_____

_____

_____

_____

_____

DAY NINETEEN
RENEWING YOUR MIND

Scriptural text: And be not conformed to this world: but be ye transformed by the renewing of your mind, that ye may prove what is that good, and acceptable, and perfect will of God (Rom. 12:2).

This text is an eye opener to admire higher realms of fulfillment. Improper conformation has a blindfolding effect. It is impossible to criticize what you believe and support. Truthfully, belief, support and attestation are products of the mind. Undoubtedly, the mind is the power house of purpose and the origin of success or failure.

Again, it is the engine room of decision making. The quality of your mind is equivalent to the quality of your life. Moreover, if your mind is captured, the entirety of your life has been captured. Liberty of the mind equals liberty of purpose. You must always bear in your heart that the battle of destiny is fought in your mind. Either knowingly or unknowingly, your mind dictates your destination.

It is clearly indicated in the scriptural text that transformation of any kind is only possible through the engagement of the mind. If your mind is not functioning well, transformation will only remain a mere dream. Therefore, you should do everything possible within your power to renew and as well rekindle the light of your mind. If you undermine your mind, you are ignorantly undermining your purpose.

That ye may prove what is that good, and acceptable, and perfect will of God.

The statement above is an excerpt from the scriptural text and it connotes purpose. Therefore, purpose can only be achieved when the mind is constantly renewed. Life is dynamic, people are unstable, and our environment is changing on daily basis. All these indicate that something needs to change within you. Needless to say, a change of mind will culminate into the change of your state and status. Inwardly, you must not be static; instead, you should be fresh and dynamic.

Reflection: For me to achieve purpose, something must change within me.

Prayer point: I receive the mind of Christ in Jesus' name.

Note:_____

_____

_____

_____

_____

_____

DAY TWENTY
BE YOURSELF

Scriptural text: But by the grace of God I am what I am: and his grace which was bestowed upon me was not in vain; but I labored more abundantly than they all: yet not I, but the grace of God which was with me. Therefore whether it were I or they, so we preach, and so ye believed (1 Cor. 15:10).

All heroines of ages past that fulfilled God's purpose for their lives knew the importance of believing in themselves. Every purpose has a special grace apportioned to it, and it is impossible to become fulfilled by ignoring your purpose, while coveting another person's purpose. Remember, you cannot find fulfillment by mimicking other people's purpose. Mimicking purpose is a fruitless effort, because you have only being empowered to become yourself.

I remember the story of a talented footballer who was unable to perform excellently in his national team because he was trying to mimic the playing style of a legend in that same team. Paul was an Apostle that did not physically walk with Jesus during His earthly ministry. Though he had several Apostles to pattern his life and ministry after, but he did otherwise. Assuming he had tried to mimic Apostle Peter, the overall leader of all Apostles, he wouldn't have fulfilled his purpose. He was the last among the Apostles, yet he evolved to become the greatest Apostle of all times.

Grace has made you a distinct woman, never try to unmake yourself, because attempting to change what God made you to be is like striving against God's plan. Besides, if you are not pleased with yourself, you are frustrating God's grace and you are technically distorting His plan and purpose.

God is great and He specializes in making good and great things. God doesn't make inferior things; rather He repeatedly crafts superior and original designs. Womanhood is not a sign of weakness; instead, it's a mark of distinction and uniqueness. There is no day a woman will metamorphose to man; therefore be your unique self.

Moreover, you should stop seeing yourself as mere subordinate. Though you may be playing the role of a subordinate in your different workplaces, however, you should always remember that no major component will function perfectly without the minor component. You are important and highly relevant in your family, church, organization and society. When people look down on you, never look down on yourself.

Reflection: If you fail to express your true personality, you may not find your real position in life.

Prayer point: Father, give me a true revelation of myself.

Note:_____

_____

_____

_____

DAY TWENTY-ONE
BE STEADFAST

Scriptural text: Therefore, my beloved brethren, be ye steadfast, unmovable, always abounding in the work of the Lord, forasmuch as ye know that your labor is not in vain in the Lord (1 Cor. 15:58).

Instability is a curse, while disloyalty is a crime. It's obvious that everybody likes loyal and stable people around them. Many people are displaced in life because of their unsteadiness.

Naturally, nobody likes to marry, relate, employ, engage, vouch or trust unsteady people. It is apparent that a wavering lifestyle will subsequently produce troubled and turbulent experience. It is impossible to experience awesome experience from oscillatory lifestyle.

Firmness, steadfastness, loyalty and sincerity are vital tools that will always boost the chance of fulfilling your goal and purpose. Women should desist from living deceptive lives. They must keep their promises and be trustworthy in their daily dealings with people. You should let your yes be yes, while your nay must remain nay. A lot of highly respected people have lost their honor because of their unstable lifestyle.

What are you known for? Don't shift if there is no significant reason to shift. Variegated lifestyle will constantly produce catastrophic results. If you are not known for something, you would not be trusted with tangible things and positions. Kindly allow people to know you for who you are.

You must constantly stay within the confine of your purpose and calling. It is imperative to stand and remain upright in your purpose. Many women carelessly lose their future and fortune to unsteadiness. You must be a woman of firm determination before you can have good delivery of your purpose.

Only stable people can successfully scale through life. It is an indisputable fact that there will be challenges as you journey through life, but your resolution and ruggedness will help you in overcoming your challenges. Be informed, inconsistency is worse than inability, therefore, be consistent.

Furthermore, don't be static in life, because continuity is synonymous with stability. You need to maintain your good work. Truly, any slight deviation from doing good work may lead to a lifetime of struggle, failure and regret. When a stable person deviates, such a person will suffer the consequence of being unstable.

Reflection: Any woman that lays her hand upon the plough and looks back is neither worthy of earthly nor eternal reward.

Prayer point: In the order of Jesus, I receive the grace to be stable and trustworthy in Jesus' name.

Note:_____

_____

_____

_____

DAY TWENTY-TWO
THE POWER OF FOCUS

Scriptural text: The light of the body is the eye: if therefore thine eye be single, thy whole body shall be full of light (Mt. 6:22).

Focus is one of the veritable ingredients of success. Broken focus often leads to broken destiny. It becomes imperative for ladies and women to stay focus in every of their endeavor and calling.

Focus unleashes conviction and consequently empowers women to pay cognizance to important things of life. Be reminded, everything in life doesn't have equal importance. Therefore, priority must be given to those things that can distinct you and add great value to your life as a woman.

And a woman having an issue of blood twelve years, which had spent all her living upon physicians, neither could be healed of any (**Lk. 8:43**).

There are several major reasons that ought to deter the woman with the issue of blood from receiving her healing; she had exhausted her money due to medical bills, she was relatively weak due to continual loss of blood and moving through the great crowd to touch Jesus' garment is almost an impossible task. This woman dared all the barriers and conquered them via the power of focus.

The power of focus has the ability to skew challenges and difficulties to ingredients of success. The life of Ruth exemplified this truth, the gloom of death encapsulated her husband and it appeared she has come to the end of herself.

Yet, she stayed focused by ignoring the idols and bounties of Moab, and cleaved to the true God of Israel. Miraculously, her difficult situation bowed to the power of her focus. Later, Ruth married a rich man; consequently, she became the great grandmother of our Lord and Savior, Jesus Christ.

As a lady, don't allow anything to steal your focus. Whatever can steal your focus can steal your success. Despite your previous disappointments and failures, if you will stay focus like the woman with the issue of blood, your marriage will work again, your career will blossom, your health will be restored, your walk with God will be revived and your finance will be greatly blessed by God.

The Holy Bible has several examples of Matriarchs of faith that you can glean and learn from their exemplary lives. Through the power of focus, Deborah delivered an entire nation from the grip of their enemies, Sarah became the mother of nations, Hannah broke the backbone of barrenness to become the mother of a national prophet, Ruth became the great grandmother of Jesus Christ, Prophetess Anna successfully prayed for the birth of Jesus and the woman with the issue of blood received her healing.

Today, as you engage the power of focus, your name will be added to the noble list above. Consequently, your spiritual walk with God, career, finance and marriage will experience a total turn around.

Reflection: Focus helps you maximize your strength and enhances your result.

Prayer point: Father, grant me the grace to stay focus in Jesus' name.

Note:_____

_____

_____

_____

_____

_____

DAY TWENTY-THREE
HARD WORK DOESN'T KILL

Scriptural text: *She riseth also while it is yet night, and giveth meat to her household, and a portion to her maidens **(Prov. 31:15).***

If God, the creator of heaven and earth could work relentlessly for six days – approximately, eighty-six percent of the week, ladies have no excuse to be lazy. Are you not created in the image and likeness of God? Hence, your disposition to work must expressly reveal that you are the daughter of the Most High God.

Be reminded, femininity is not synonymous with laziness; instead, femininity is synonymous with profitable investment of strength and meaningful engagement of skills and virtue. The account of the virtuous woman succinctly described in the Book of Proverbs Chapter thirty-one, leaves no woman with an excuse to be lazy.

A woman is an epitome of strength and productivity. When God was to introduce woman in the Book of Genesis, the word "help" employed by God, perfectly described the usefulness, functionality and office of women.

God was not haphazard about the creation of woman. He couldn't have made a lazy being (gender) as help meet for the man. God in His indescribable wisdom partnered with the womb of a woman for procreation and engaged her awesomely built nature to stabilize the home. Indeed, womanhood is a hard work. However, hard work does not kill; it only prepares you for a glorious and rewarding future.

It must be noted that when women fail to discharge their responsibilities, the resultant effects may include; unstable home, godless children, reckless society and beggarly nation.

Though the demand on a woman appears unending; a child trainer, care giver, home builder, career person and mother of nation, all at once is a herculean task. But you must realize that God has bestowed the office of woman with adequate and efficient grace to dutifully perform her role.

Despite being sons of a priest, Hophni and Phinehas lived reckless and godless lives. This is traceable to the fact that their mother was largely passive or totally inactive in their training. When woman's role as a trainer is missing, the society, church and nation will inevitably suffer it.

The virtuous woman in the Book of Proverbs is a perfect template for every woman to emulate and model their lives after. Her life echoed how relevant a woman should be; a wife, mother, investor, societal model, home keeper and manager.

Whenever a woman sees her God-given roles as a disturbance, such a woman is a failure and insensitive to her divine calling. Therefore, let all women ask for divine grace to effectively fulfill their roles as wives, mothers, career women and other facets of their ministries.

Reflection: The failure of a woman has a ripple effect on the society. Diligently play your God-given roles.

Prayer points: I receive grace to succeed in my God-given roles as a woman.

Note:_____

_____

_____

_____

_____

_____

DAY TWENTY-FOUR
LEAN ON GOD

Scriptural text: I will lift up mine eyes unto the hills, from whence cometh my help. My help cometh from the Lord, which made heaven and earth (Ps. 121:1-2).

Like men, women have their limitations; hence, the need to lean on God for support and strength. Evidently, there is no woman that can help herself without the help of God. Trying to help oneself outside of God is a sign of arrogance and God opposes the proud, but He gives grace to the humble.

Women must know that there is no difficult case with God. Therefore, regardless of what you are experiencing, be informed that God can intervene and change your mess to a message. Sarah must have been disregarded and branded the emblem of barrenness, but God caused her to give birth at age 90. Esther was a mere slave in Shushan, but God intervened and enthroned her as queen. Mary was a virgin, yet God partnered with her womb to do the seemingly impossible. Without conjugation, she gave birth to the Savior of the world – Jesus Christ.

"…Be it unto me according to thy word…" **(Lk. 1:38).**

It is imperative for all women to have total reliance on God. She accepted the decision of heaven and was ready to bear whatever consequence comes alongside her reliance on God.

Truthfully, God is too faithful to fail. Biblical records and history books are full of people who trusted God enough to lean on Him. Amazingly, God made them signs and wonders to their world.

Deborah was just an ordinary house wife, but she trusted God enough, consequently, she became an unforgettable heroine. Through her hands, the Lord gave peace and rest to the children of Israel.

In your case, you can become another Deborah of your nation and family. You can conquer the enemies of your marriage, finance, career, health and ministry. God will jealously guard the interest of those who lean on Him. Leaning on God exempts you from general failure and pain experienced by other women.

Women who have mastered the art of leaning on God via prayer, fasting and godly service are great assets to their family members. Despite the foolishness of Nabal, Abigail was able to protect him with her responsive giving and plea to King David.

Trust in the LORD with all your heart, and lean not on your own understanding; in all your ways acknowledge Him, and He shall direct your paths **(Prov. 3:5-6).**

There is a way that seems right, ensure you lean on God and not your intuition. The fact a way looks good doesn't make it good. The forbidden fruit looked good, Eve ate and gave it to Adam, and consequently, they were cursed. Sarah's advice to Abraham about her maid looked good, but the world has not recovered from the damage of her careless advice. Lot's wife thought it was a good idea to reexamine her lost properties; pathetically, she became a pillar of salt.

As a woman, lean on God at all times and you will be amazed by the jaw-dropping results that will accompany your life.

Reflection: failure to lean on God is a sign of arrogance and pride; eventually, it will be punished by God.

Prayer point: I receive the grace to totally lean on God in Jesus' name.

Note:_____

_____

_____

_____

_____

_____

DAY TWENTY-FIVE
ALWAYS PANT FOR KNOWLEDGE

Scriptural text: And when the queen of Sheba heard of the fame of Solomon concerning the name of the Lord, she came to prove him with hard questions. And she came to Jerusalem with a very great train, with camels that bare spices, and very much gold, and precious stones: and when she was come to Solomon, she communed with him of all that was in her heart (1 Kg. 10:1-2).

It is wiser to seek knowledge than money. Queen of Sheba knew this truth, and on the strength of this, she came to King Solomon to learn from him. Evidently, she returned to her land wiser than when she visited, because those who truly seek wisdom finds it and their lives are testimonials of the excellence of wisdom.

Interestingly, no woman is an island of knowledge. Always, there is something you can learn from other people that can bring stability and harmony to your home. For example, learning how to cook a particular delicacy, home economics and management training can spice your home with happiness in a great way. If the Queen of Sheba could leave her palace in search of wisdom, then, there is no sacrifice that is too much to make in your quest for knowledge.

Through wisdom is a house builded; and by understanding it is established (**Prov. 24:3**).

The building blocks used in building a loving home is wisdom. Regardless of how intelligent a woman is, she must also learn from other women. Sometimes, knowledge can be acquired from attending seminars, conferences, workshops, reading books, watching videos and several other platforms of learning.

When the Pharisees were loudly communicating their naivety, Jesus asked them an important question, "Have you not read?" Truthfully, many of the marital problems and challenges experienced by couples are clear indications that they have not been panting for knowledge.

The time has come for women to see themselves as major players in their families and societies. However, you cannot give what you don't have. Only women who have panted and acquired sufficient knowledge can administer leadership and experience success in their assorted endeavors.

Despite being our Savior and Lord, Jesus Christ paid adequate attention to knowledge acquisition. At age twelve, Jesus was asking questions and listening to doctors of law. No wonder, He flawlessly defeated Satan when he tempted Him.

A wise man once said, "There is no mountain anywhere, the ignorance of every woman is her mountain". Every woman must destroy her own mountain of ignorance by panting for knowledge in the order of the Queen of Sheba.

Graciously, we probably wouldn't have known about Queen of Sheba if not for her insatiable quest for knowledge. Similarly, when you develop a healthy desire to know and understand things, your relevance will grow at an amazing rate.

Reflection: When you stop learning, then, you start dying.

Prayer point: Father, grant me the spirit of wisdom, knowledge and understanding in Jesus' name.

Note:_____

_____

_____

_____

_____

_____

DAY TWENTY-SIX
RIGHTEOUSNESS EXALTS

Scriptural text: *Righteousness exalteth a nation: but sin is a reproach to any people* ***(Prov. 14:34)***

The Scripture cannot be broken, because God is the keeper of His laws. Despite being God's own covenant people, the disobedience of Achan affected the entire nation of Israel. Unfortunately, the small nation of Ai put the soldiers of Israel to flight. This defeat was a major setback for the traveling nation of Israel. Eventually, Achan and his family members were destroyed. Afterwards, God was pacified and His anger turned away from His people.

Every unconfessed act of unrighteousness demotes. This is so because God is the lifter of all things – human beings, nations, organizations, etc. Truthfully, God is of purer eyes; hence, He cannot behold iniquity. Immediately an act of unrighteousness is committed, God and His power that lifts will drawback. This will give room for failure, suffering, pain and demotion of whoever has committed such unrighteous act.

Thus saith the Lord, behold, I will raise up evil against thee out of thine own house, and I will take thy wives before thine eyes, and give them unto thy neighbor, and he shall lie with thy wives in the sight of this sun. For thou didst it secretly: but I will do this thing before all Israel, and before the sun ***(2 Sam 12:11-12).***

King David, despite being a man after God's heart, when he drifted into sin and took Bathsheba, God's punishment landed on him. His leadership was greatly affected, because of his sin, enemies rose up against him and this dark moment of his life seemed unending until God intervened.

It becomes imperative for all women to know that it doesn't matter if the unrighteous act was committed in secret. God can see through the thickest darkness and there is no secret before God. Joseph knew this truth, despite the sweetened and convincing words of the wife of Portiphar, Joseph called it "Great wickedness." He knew that God will see and punish such act of unrigteousness.

And Pharaoh said unto Joseph, See, I have set thee over all the land of Egypt **(Gen. 41:41).**

Eventually, Joseph's righteousness lifted him from the pit of prison to an envious position in Egypt. Though he suffered the pains of false allegation and imprisonment, but in one day God gave Joseph a major breakthrough. Without a stressful campaign, he became the second-in-command to Pharaoh and he was given Pharaoh's ring, vesture of linen, gold chain and royal chariot. Graciously, Potipherah gave her daughter to Joseph as wife – all in one day.

Sincerely, the price of living a righteous life is huge, but the aftermath effects are worthy, far rewarding and greatly profitable. Often times, the unrighteous may appears to be making speedy progress, but remember that the unrighteousness of Cain made him a vagabond, Haman crashed from royalty to an ignoble state, Jezebel lost her position and became food for dogs, Nebuchadnezzar lived like an animal for seven years, Herod was eaten by worms and Judas Iscariot dug his untimely grave.

Women must endeavor to live righteous lives, because that is a sure way of been promoted by God. Amidst all odds, ensure that your daily activities, relationships, career dealings, financial transactions and services rendered are such that glorifies God.

Never make empty claims that the challenges now are more than ever, this is not true. People of different dispensations have different monster of unrighteousness to conquer. Quit making excuses, confront and conquer the monster of fornication, adultery, unfaithfulness, corruption, recklessness and other foxes that can spoil your vine. Consider this, despite the palpable godlessness of Sodom, Lot's daughters were virgins. Stop complaining, instead, call for God's grace today.

Reflection: Righteousness is a ladder of promotion, while unrighteousness is a miry pit of demotion.

Prayer points: Father, empower me to live a righteous life.

Note:_____

_____

_____

_____

_____

_____

DAY TWENTY-SEVEN
FIGHT THE GOOD FIGHT OF FAITH

Scriptural text: *Fight the good fight of faith, lay hold on eternal life, whereunto thou art also called, and hast professed a good profession before many witnesses (1 Tim. 6:12).*

T he story of Lot's wife must always remind all women that God has definite expectations concerning their lives. One of such expectations is fighting the good fight of faith. Expectedly, without faith, it is impossible to please God, because faith is the only currency with which valid and legitimate transactions can be made with God.

Please be informed, faith is not a masculine character. Therefore, it is imperative for women to grow and become women of faith. Faith is a veritable weapon of spiritual warfare; it will work for whoever engages it with understanding. Deborah didn't change her gender before she led the children of Israel to victory. Queen Esther had faith in God of Israel, after praying and fasting, God used her to play a pivotal role in stopping the annihilation of the Jews.

Like Deborah and Esther, the victory you desire to see in your marriage, ministry, career, finance and other endeavors of life can only come by fighting a good fight of faith. The realities of the 21st century have made it so clear that enviable success cannot be gotten by doubters.

Only women of faith, courage, determination and strong will are making waves in science, politics, ministry, education, business, etc. Faith confers victory both in the spiritual and physical realms. Rahab was a woman of faith, and her faith precipitated the deliverance of her family members from the destruction that befell Jericho.

Above all, taking the shield of faith, wherewith ye shall be able to quench all the fiery darts of the wicked (Eph. 6:16).

Apostle Paul placed faith above all other weapons of spiritual warfare highlighted in Ephesians Chapter six. This is not a mistake; every other weapon can only be efficiently utilized when faith is in place. Graciously, Apostle Paul made it clear that the shield of faith can quench all darts of the wicked. The word "all" means everything without exception.

What is confronting your marriage and giving you sleepless night? What is inhibiting your career and making it seems you are not good enough? What are the impediments challenging your ministerial advancements? Which sickness has made life unbearable for you? Apostle Paul made it clear that the weapon called faith can quench all the fiery darts of the wicked listed above.

Then, why hang your head in pain when the solution is available? It is time to fight the good fight of faith that will deliver your desired success, victory, growth and accomplishment. Stop wasting your precious time crying and feeling depressed. Forcefully banish Satan out of the territory of your mind using the weapon of faith. Pity party will not help your destiny, call it off. It is time to stamp your feet on the ground and say, "I will fight the good fight of faith", and God will honor your faith and give you jaw-dropping conquest.

Reflection: If doubt will not help you, why not fight the good fight of faith?

Prayer point: Father, as I fight the good fight of faith, I recover all that I have lost to doubt and Satan in Jesus' name.

Note:_____

_____

_____

_____

_____

_____

DAY TWENTY-EIGHT
FAILURE IS NOT FINAL

Scriptural text: *For a just man falleth seven times, and riseth up again: but the wicked shall fall into mischief* ***(Prov. 24:16).***

Regardless of the number of times you have fallen, you can rise again. Failures are indicators that there are certain things you haven't properly learned. Therefore, never stop learning the important lessons that are required in gaining mastery in your chosen field.

Undoubtedly, failure is one of the most proficient liars of all times. It will try to convince you that it is the last bus station, but be informed, if you can look ahead, you are few meters away from achieving notable success. Being a liar, failure has mastered the art of employing difficult situations, unfriendly friends, unloving relatives, financial hardship, disturbing allegations and mockers of purpose to convince you that all hope is lost.

Job's wife perfectly exhibited this evil trait. She concluded in her heart that her husband cannot recover from his failure. Therefore, she advised her husband to curse God and die. Please note, failure will make it seems that cursing God and dying is better than trusting and waiting on God. Like Job, stamp your feet on the ground and say, "I know that my redeemer lives."

If God can restore all that Job lost; his investment, children and health, then, be informed, your failure is just a fleeting phase and it will definitely pass. Surely, your challenges will turn around to a testimony.

It is also important you understand that the opinions of humans can be venomous to your recovery process from failure to success. Therefore, respect people and their opinions, but do what you consider right and good for you. Do you know that people don't really expect you to rise from your fallen state? They call you names that reflect their thoughts. Interestingly, do you know that Rahab later had an encounter with the God of Israel? Yet people call her Rahab the harlot. Bartimaeus was not blind forever, yet people call him blind Bartimaeus.

In your case they might have labeled you barren, unemployed, sick, dull, ugly, obese, poor or failure, but don't make it messier by responding to your critics and naysayers. Instead, let your Jaw-dropping results answer them.

There is an important lesson to learn from Jesus. After his death and burial, He was not arguing or debating with anyone. But when they went to visit His tomb on the third day, they met an empty tomb. Result speaks better and louder than argument.

Do not agree with naysayers. Like they did to Jesus, they probably had killed and bury you with their scorching words, negative conclusions and damaging allegations. Also act like Jesus, the tomb (failure) is not the final place, there is resurrection (success) ahead of you.

Truly, failure is not final, you can succeed again. If Esther did not die as a slave, you will rule and reign. If Joseph did not die in the prison, you will become a global solution giver. If Mary Magdalene did not die as a demon possessed woman, fresh and mighty power of the Holy Spirit of the Lord will come upon your life.

Always tell yourself, no negative event is potent enough to limit my destiny. This failure is not my end, but a precursor of success. I am not a failure, because the anointing of success is upon my life. Therefore, always arm yourself with this truth, failure is not final, success is my portion.

Reflection: There is resurrection after death; I will rise from my failure to achieve jaw-dropping success.

Prayer point: Father, anoint me with the grace to succeed in every endeavor of life.

Note:_____

_____

_____

_____

_____

_____

DAY TWENTY-NINE
IT SHALL COME TO PASS

Scriptural text: And it shall come to pass afterward, that I will pour out my Spirit upon all flesh; and your sons and your daughters shall prophesy, your old men shall dream dreams, your young men shall see visions (Joel 2:28).

God is faithful concerning every of his promise. Whatever God has promised you, He has the ability to fulfill it. Through His servant, Prophet Joel, God promised that He will release His Spirit upon all flesh and there was a fulfillment of this promise in the book of Acts Chapter two, verses two to four.

And suddenly there came a sound from heaven as of a rushing mighty wind, and it filled all the house where they were sitting. And there appeared unto them cloven tongues like as of fire, and it sat upon each of them. And they were all filled with the Holy Ghost, and began to speak with other tongues, as the Spirit gave them utterance (Act 2:2-4).

Be reminded, God has not forgotten His promises concerning your purpose. The plans He has for you are plans of good and not of evil, to give you a glorious future. God has the ability to bring to pass whatever He has promised you.

And it came to pass, when Joseph was come unto his brethren, that they stripped Joseph out of his coat, his coat of many colors that was on him; and they took him, and cast him into a pit: and the pit was empty, there was no water in it **(Gen. 37:23-24).**

Joseph was surrounded by enemies; his glorious destiny wore a gloomy garb. It appeared his destiny was drifting to obscurity. He moved from slavery to prison and from pain to greater pain. False allegation incarcerated him to prison for about thirteen years, but one glorious day, God's purpose for his life came to pass.

For the vision is yet for an appointed time, but at the end it shall speak, and not lie: though it tarry, wait for it; because it will surely come, it will not tarry **(Hab. 2:3).**

However, you must know that every purpose is subjected to divine timing. A fertile egg doesn't hatch before the required time, if it does, it will die. God doesn't want your purpose to die, because as it is in the natural, so it is in the supernatural. Your purpose must obey the law of time, because there is time for every purpose under heaven.

And he said, I will certainly return unto thee according to the time of life; and, lo, Sarah thy wife shall have a son. And Sarah heard it in the tent door, which was behind him **(Gen. 18:10).**

It is worthy to glean and learn a golden lesson from the encounter Sarah had with the heavenly visitors. These divine delegates have the power to make Sarah conceive and give birth in a day or shorter time, but they did otherwise. They subjected Sarah's fruitfulness to the irrefutable law of time, "According to the time of life."

Is it a time to receive money, and to receive garments, and oliveyards, and vineyards, and sheep, and oxen, and menservants, and maidservants? (2 kg 5:26).

Dear woman, learn from the misdemeanor of Gehazi, he ran ahead of time and his purpose crashed in a disturbing manner. He got leprosy instead of double portion anointing. Prophet Elisha asked Gehazi a notable question which your purpose must equally answer, "Is it a time...?"

If it is not your time, your purpose cannot find expression. You must learn how to wait on God and perfectly align with His will for your life. Through the thick and thin of persecution, David waited on God. Eventually, after his third coronation, God establish his kingdom.

Whatever challenge you are experiencing at the moment, they are your cave of Adullam, such challenge will bring out the giant in you. The earthly ministry of Jesus Christ was a success, because His purpose perfectly aligned with the divine timing of God for His life and ministry. Consider this amazing truth; the foundation of Jesus' three-and-half year's ministry was laid for thirty solid years.

God is not haphazard in any of His dealings, and He won't start with you. He is committed to bringing to pass all of His promises concerning your purpose. However, you must learn the principle of time, training and diligence. Never doubt God, everything He has promised you will come to pass.

While trusting Him for fulfillment, ensure you wait profitably by honing your skills, acquiring more certificates and training. At the fullness of time, all of His promises will come to pass.

Reflection: Has God ever disappointed anyone before? No! He won't start with you, belief Him wholeheartedly, because He is faithful.

Prayer point: I receive grace to wait profitably like the five wise virgins in Jesus' name.

Note:_____

_____

_____

_____

_____

_____

DAY THIRTY
KEEP PRESSING

Scriptural text: *I press toward the mark for the prize of the high calling of God in Christ Jesus* **(Phil 3:14).**

Continual pressing is the fuel of every glorious destiny. Nothing kills purpose faster than undue satisfaction and untimely gratification. Apostle Paul knew this truth and he intelligently devised a sound method of disregarding his laudable achievements in order to keep pressing.

Those who build monuments from their achievements often miss out on the opportunity for greater exploits. What would have happened if God rested after the first day of creation? What would have happened if Moses only stayed with God on Mount Sinai for a day? What would have happened if Daniel had stopped praying when his answer was hindered? What would have happened if Jesus started celebrating His first miracle – at Cana of Galilee? What would have happened if the disciples left the upper room after praying for one day? What would have happened if Apostle Paul had stopped pressing after he wrote his first epistle?

One notable weakness of our generation is that we celebrate too early. In other words, we are the "Celebrating generation", consequently, we have missed out on the invaluable benefits of pressing more.

If our generation were to be the traveling nation of Israel that crossed the red sea; we would still be throwing party and taking 'selfie' only to be overtaken and captured by the Egyptian soldiers again.

Which of your achievements have dug a pit of limitation around your life? You must fill the pit up today and press for more success, anointing, wisdom, enlightenment and mystery.

And went after the man of God, and found him sitting under an oak: and he said unto him, art thou the man of God that camest from Judah? And he said, I am (1 Kg. 13:14).

The genesis of the fall of the young Prophet was his decision to rest when he ought to return to where he came from. Consequently, the old deceiving Prophet convinced him to return with him. Finally, he became a prey to Lion.

Have you noticed that rivers with high flowing rate have higher purity than stagnant body of water – lake? Stagnant water stinks; similarly, women who stop pressing will soon become irrelevant to their society, church, family and nation.

Like Apostle Paul, women with glorious destiny must learn how to forge ahead despite their laudable achievements, feats and successes. This was the rebuke God gave to Joshua, informing him that there are more lands to conquer. In your case there are more children, contracts, certificates, conferences, workshops and exposure to get. Don't settle in Goshen, there is a land flowing with milk and honey and God is set to take you there.

Reflection: Don't settle for a tent, because there is a palace prepared for you.

Prayer points: O Lord, I receive grace to press for the higher prize of my calling in Jesus' name.

Note:_____

_____

_____

_____

_____

_____

DAY THIRTY-ONE
SHUN EVIL ASSOCIATION

Scriptural text: Be not deceived: evil communications corrupt good manners (1 Cor. 15:33).

Association is potent enough to make or mar any destiny. It was not recorded in the Bible that the wife of Lot was living a sinful life, but her association with Sodom spelt her doom in a pathetic manner.

Apostle Peter became eternally relevant because of his association with Jesus. At most, he would have ended up as the best fisherman in Galilee. Surprisingly, there is no fisherman whose name featured in the Holy Bible. Suffice to say, if Apostle Peter had not associated with Jesus, nobody would have known him.

Association can be a ladder to greatness, and conversely, it can be a drifting rail to perdition. The untimely death of Sapphira was solely inspired by her association with Ananias. Forty two children were consumed by two bears when they formed an evil alliance to mock Prophet Elisha.

Be informed, association is not mandatory, hence, women must carefully select the kind of association they keep. The grave consequence of sinful association is inexplicable; so many people become victims of their choices and never recover.

For as many as are led by the Spirit of God, they are the sons of God (Rom. 8:14).

There are several people who have taken the issue of association casually, and in no distant time, they became casualties. It becomes imperative to be led by God at all times. Despite being the son of God, Jesus prayed and was led by God while choosing His disciples. If Jesus was not casual about the people He associated with, then, you must realize that there is a way that seems right, but the end is destruction.

Women must ensure that they shun evil association at all cost, as this can adversely affect their marriage, career, ministry, finance and health. Evidently, an evil associate will give evil advice. Evil associate sank the destiny of Amnon, and his untimely death was traceable to the advice given to him by Jonadab. The cancerous effect of evil association is chain-like and grievous. In the case of Amnon, an evil advice led to the defilement of Tamar, and ultimately to the cruel assassination of Amnon by Absalom.

When we allow the word of God to guide us, we will enter into profitable association like that of Moses and Aaron, David and Jonathan, Daniel and the three Hebrews, Paul and Silas and other associations recorded in the Holy Bible which enhanced intimacy with God, exhibited the power of love and teaches us several invaluable lessons.

Finally, your eyes, experience and feelings have their limitations, they cannot accurately guide you into having a godly and profitable association. Lot, the brother of Abraham fell in love with the vegetation of Sodom. Unfortunately, he left Sodom with painful scars. Mistakenly, when you find yourself associating with wrong people, you should be quick to retrace your step. Lot later realized how wicked the people of Sodom was, but he didn't make plan to relocate. If not for the mercy of God and intercession of Abraham, he would have probably lost his life and family to the fiery inferno of heaven poured upon Sodom and Gomorrah.

Reflection: Association is powerful; it can dictate your earthly relevance and eternal destiny.

Prayer point: Father, I receive the grace to discern the right people that will add value to my life

Note:_____

_____

_____

_____

_____

_____